Famil

GW01066279

"Cluck, cluck!
Cluck, cluck!"

"Hello, Mother Hen.
How many chicks
do you have?"

"Madam, I have ten."

"Hiss, hiss!
Hiss, hiss!"

"How are you,
Mother Goose?
Where have your
six goslings gone?"

"Madam, they're
on the loose."

"Ai-oga! Ai-oga!"

"Hi there, Father Swan.
I came to feed your family.
Where have your cygnets gone?"

14

"Three of them are diving.
Three of them are in the nest.
Three of them are paddling back.
That makes nine of the best!"

3 + 3 + 3 = 9

"Shoo, shoo! Shoo, shoo!
You have all been fed.
It's time to feed my children
and tuck them into bed."